Saints of the Republic

Chip Livingston

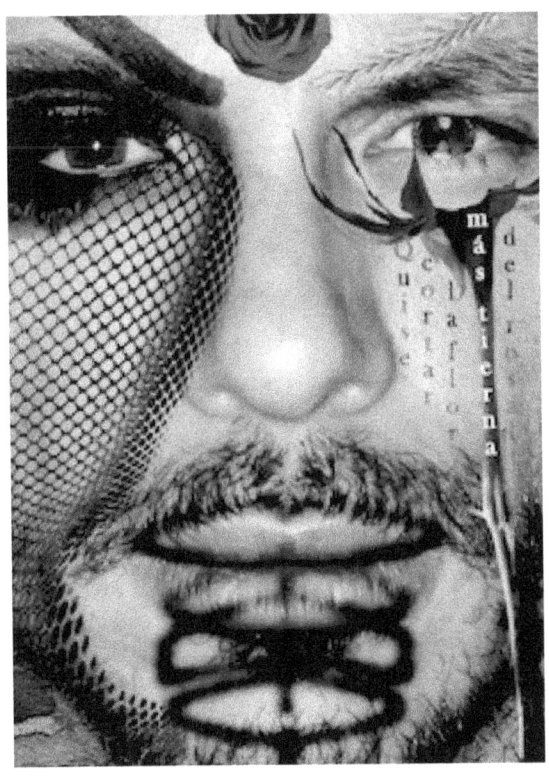

SPUYTEN DUYVIL

New York   Paris

ISBN 978-1-959556-02-2

Library of Congress Cataloging-in-Publication Data

Names: Livingston, Chip, author.
Title: Saints of the republic / Chip Livingston.
Description: New York : Spuyten Duyvil, [2023]
Identifiers: LCCN 2022053656 | ISBN 9781959556022 (paperback)
Subjects: LCGFT: Poetry.
Classification: LCC PS3612.I953 S25 2023 | DDC 811/.6--dc23/eng/20221114
LC record available at https://lccn.loc.gov/2022053656

for the lovers

PART III   SAINTS OF THE REPUBLIC

Acknowledgments

PART I
SANTOS DE LA REPÚBLICA

Palo Borracho

The jacaranda blooms beside the drunk stick tree.
Come. I see you swell with nectar. Hear you,
Venteveos, shriek till night. "Come. See me."
The jacaranda blooms beside the drunk stick tree.
The violent violet petals pollen weep.
A bichofeo sings of you with open throat and beak.
The jacaranda blooms beside the drunk stick tree.
I see you swell with nectar, hear you shriek.

SAN BENITO

the black bird stripped off their feathers
they issued the jubilee of plenary indulgence
in eucharistic communion expressing effects
of anxieties intercessed and intersexed

the black bird stripped off their feathers
and threw themselves into a thicket of thorns
protected by presence of viper and crown
a sacramental medal of uncertain origin

the poison was offered the glass was broken
they issued the jubilee of plenary indulgence
the black bird stripped off their feathers

San Vitalis of Fetishes

If I preserve your head in the water from your own cistern,
would you be my Piss Christ, expiate my sins immoral and numerous?
They are licentious, San Vitalis, a cross between my legs.

After pilgrimaging your sanctuaries, attending baptisms stern,
I possessed my reputation contained, took my eucharist.
Gluttoning miraculous elixirs, my hermitage turned,
metamorphosing my whispers vesuvius.
You were licentious, San Vitalis, you put your cross between my legs,

generated pentecost by turning my head glorious, address
in the clouds. Assimilating various oddities a holiness returns.
We are licentious, San Vitalis, my cross between your legs.

SAN TIMOTHEOS' LINE

ordained we companion congregations

         / of timid affections

Saint Timothy

        \ dear and faithful

              child
              disciple
              helper
              companion

                     \ of Paul

I have no one like you

        / under Diana's stone

No other

        \ has spread such gospel

             rightful \
     ordaining   companions

     by the laying

        \ on of hands

```
        / swallow the eucharist
You     – take the spit
        \ never turn your back



              / share the host
Timotheos = you
              \ share the laying-on of hands
```

Santos de la República

There have been so many gods I've loved
My sex is devoted, dedicated to Eros
Excessive examinations religious and secular

There are so many gods to love
Interpreting exaltations celestial
A musing of muses as saints feast and famine

The miracle witnessed of corporal mammon
My text is devotion dedication to Eros
There are so many gods I love

Las Llamadas

jealousy leads me to the parade
applause to the boot shuffle

a heart off   a heart on
summoned by my interweaving

a pendant against the extended dancer
I twirl the flag   I kiss the leather sequined jewel

I shimmy off the hundredth so-called imperfection

my headdress is a kind of production
erect and eager tongues

stilt-walking a fault line
the tame curtsy a red herring

I take a knee
skating time and light

a tongue on
          until the hold is believed
                    a tongue off

boom cha cha cha
boom cha cha cha ta ta ta ta ta ta ta ta

San Judas Tadeo, Apostle of God's Image

my \
Patron of   > holy imagination
un /

                    un \   / ed
Pastor of inhibitions   bound
                    a /   \ s

                / visioned   carbon \
Emissionary   in   un   dated
                            \ covered

Protector \
              >   San Tadeo Jesus' kept
Protected /

                                        / of
    / safekeeper   / kingdom   > rest
My   my   my   \ un
              \ keepsake

                                    / confess

San Judas Tadeo to thee I

                            \ un

                                    > dress

                        ad

                    / locked

A kiss un   imagined as woodsmoke

                    re /

                                    / musket-rubbed

Petitioned & adored   – salt-barreled   > flint

                            \ hand-cannoned

                        as   \

San Judas Tadeo   > cendant

                    des /

                                            / of God's image

Apostled & exhibitioned guardian

                                        \ San Tadeo

Sans Justus, The Martyrs

we natural sons in the love of romans
we the right guardians to address
our investigations, the superstitious
long-quote impossible reasons

such that each demon that takes us
condemns us – we looked cut
we looked curly we looked wicked
our wickedness our pious utterances just

judges' questions leading to diversions
named and corrupted, we denied
sacrifices men consider required
appetites, needs, scattered, everlasting

our wills locked not to feed fires not to feed
no kingdoms fixed no lives denied no wrong
flowers formed no denim touched
no persuaded inquiry our gods would fear

we learn nothing means decency, fear
punishes exploration of persons enshrined
our view of man knows truth forbids naming
those corrupted words struck stuck anonymous

we father the martyrs' confessions
our faiths prove many-formed

THE ALPHABET OF THE REPUBLIC

Always I'm asked what I love about Uruguay.

Because the food, I say, because the people. Because the rhythm of the place, the

Culture. *Carnaval. Candombe*

Drums that demand I dance. It's different:

Everything. Its Education – free through university and evidently effective. Everyone seems wise, well-read, self-possessed, and worldly. It's egalitarian. And though I know one Richie Rich, the majority of people are equal. They treat each other as equals. It's

Fun, I mean, *fatal*, just

Going to the grocery store, a walk in my

Hawaianas to practice my *holas*. The Healthcare – universal, modern, and fucking fantastic.

Iemanja, the goddess of the ocean. Idea (Vilariño), the first poet whose collected works I read entirely in Spanish.

Jacarandas.

Karaoke at Il Tempo. *Kioskos* to buy my tobacco *y hojillas.*

Loros, the small green parrots that top the *palmeras.*

Llaves antiguas – old skeleton keys that open our doors, and, oh man, the beautiful doors of Uruguay. There are photo books and collage posters of *las puertas* in Montevideo. I take

Mate at *merienda*, I

Nap at *siesta*,

Obey the rhythms of my borrowed land.

Public transportation. Public wifi. Public Welfare. Public exercise equipment. Institutions that actually serve the public.

Queso. I guess it makes sense that if Uruguay has the most natural beef in the world, its dairy would be as pure. Quince paste, which they call *membrillo*, and I have a story about that for another time.

Really it's remarkable I haven't mentioned the meat.

Rrrreally rrrremarkable but

Seriously, Uruguay outlawed antibiotics and hormones in its livestock in the 1970s, it's banned Monsanto and GMOs, imported

Transgenic foods are marked with a yellow triangled T. Tomatoes still taste like tomatoes in

Uruguay; bananas still have seeds. It's a long trip south but

Vale la pena. Now if I shortened "*vale la pena*" to just "*vale*," it would suggest I'm from Spain. The abridged version in Uruguay is "*dale*," used like "okay," *pero ta,*

You know I love learning these distinctions between spellings and *palabras*.

Zorrilla. Zorrilla's on the twenty-peso bill, which you can imagine as a dollar, Juan Zorrilla de San Martin, an epic Uruguayan poet, whose home, bought by scholars of the state, is now a national museum; a street and park are named for him. Juana de Ibarbourou appears on the thousand peso, a novelist and poet. The hundred peso note features Eduardo Fabini, a musician and composer. Do you know what I'm getting at? The Uruguayan money has artists and thinkers on it. And I think about the killers I carried in my U.S. wallet.

Zumba, my first onomatopoetic Spanish word, the drowsy bee's buzz.

Yerba Mate, obviously, if you know me. I've nearly always got a mate full of *yerba*, the Guaraní herb that motors the world's most nocturnal country, Uruguay.

Xcept Uruguay isn't really the country's name. *No tiene nombre oficial* but is officially known as La República Oriental del Uruguay, the republic east of the Uruguay River, referencing itself by location, by the X on the upside-down map, and uses the indigenous name of the nearby river, this cattle country crossed and bordered by rivers and sea, its bays a sweet and salty mix,

Which are just some of why and what I love about this watery *paisito*, the first time I met her crossing the Río de la Plata from Buenos Aires, on a whim, a mention, just the first weekend of a 10-day escape from North American winter with another U.S. writer. We decided within 24 hours to stay the entire holiday in Uruguay.

Verdad. Era verano. It was summer in our wintertime. *Carnaval.* And we toured the Atlantic beaches, convinced we'd been secreted into a kind of heaven, as if the *venteveos* saw and sung to us, the *velas* lit for Iemanja an extraordinary riverside welcome, warm beacons with carnations, coins, watermelons. *Y acá volvimos, vivíamos, y yo vivo de nuevo.*

Uruguay. Uruguay. Uruguay.
"Ur-u-guay? You're a guy?"
"Ur-u-guay? You're a gay?"
You're a single gay guy living in Uruguay? *Uuuuu Che! Que suerte!*

Ta! It's *tranquilo,* and truth be told, *todavía no sé* what it is to be exact. *Todo: los tomates, las tortas fritas, el tortugon. Los teros, el tango, los tambores.* The drum groups in the streets, the people on their feet, the two beats that keep the culture dancing. *Los tambores. Los tangueros.* The tango. The *tambores.* And *los Tupamaros.*

Spanish as a second language. I'd studied a semester with a Spaniard, had Cuban friends teach me to cuss, heard my share of Puerto Rican pillow talk, but learning to speak Uruguayan Spanish, *No es poca cosa, Che. No es Catalán, cierto, pero casi Canario,* an *idioma* of opposites, where a former prison is now a luxury shopping mall and the current prison is called Libertad, where barbaric and fatal are adjectives for amazing, where to experience joy is to die or to be killed by something. *Sino es así, no? O sí? Sí no?* See?

RR. Errrrrrrrre. Mi perrita, mi porro, mi ferrocarril. Mi fat yankee tongue trying to roll the double *RR. Joderrrrrrrr!*

The Rambla: among my first and constant appreciations, Montevideo's Rambla is 13.7 miles of uninterrupted sidewalk along the river and up the Atlantic coast; it's where Montevideanos ramble, rest, relax, and meet for *mate,* to read, to exercise, to take sun, run. Its rhythms still and accelerate me. *Requesón.*

Que tal? How's it going? *Quizás* you're wondering how much love for this little country I'm going to share. I'll try to be quicker.

Pero el problema es you can't rush a Uruguayan, and I am growing more *Yorugua* every day, and there are a lot of things I love in the republic that start with P: poets, there are so many poets in Uruguay, and the people actually read poetry. There are poems etched in marble in public plazas. The people read! And the people are kind, helpful, pretty and peaceful – until it comes to *fútbol*, then it's back to the killing metaphors. But *Pizza. Pasta. Pan de Azúcar*, where I saw a live wild black puma in a sheep pasture. Ah, population statistics: there are seven sheep for every human in Uruguay and there are four cows for each person. *Palermo. Piriapolis. Parque Rodó. Cabo Polonio. Punta del Diablo. Palos borachos.*

Olímpicos and other sandwiches *de miga. Las ondas buenas, ojalá, y obvio* eating

Ñoquis on the 29th of every month.

Niños envueltos, delicious sausage in cabbage with a tortuous name, wrapped children. *Riquísimos son.*

Mira! Mate, mimos, mercados, murgas, the meat (see "Carne"), *medialunas* at *merienda*, the extra meal. They have four meals a day in Uruguay! And *merienda* suits me, soothes *mi hambre* at North American dinnertime. I have to mention Pepe Mujica, the former president, his example, history, and his changing the face of the republic to *el mundo*.

Lluvia. I love the fucking rain in Uruguay and it's a good thing because this country is elemental, water falling into water, sky and sea, sea and earth, *sol* and sky, where *Las Llamadas* call me to my feet for their *ensayas y desfiles.*

Lemeyun, and I'm even allergic to onions, but this Armenian-inspired Uruguayan dish is like, *paf!,* a grilled pita bread topped with citrus spiced beef ceviche.

Kisses – abundant as bread – and everything starts and ends with a *beso.* How tender and wholesome and masculine and shattering of macho North American stereotypes of how two humans can so naturally touch each other. Granted this is one kiss on the cheek, but there are exponential expressions of their comfort with intimacy.

JAJAJA is how they text laughter. *Y les gusta reir.* And I laugh at how distant my language just got when I wrote of showing affection. I have a lot to learn yet. *Jamón y queso. Juas?*

Iemanja, I have mentioned, an important figure in my knowing the country and my gratitude. Part of my introduction,

How we arrived the first time the weekend of her birthday, February 2, and joined Montevideo on Playa Ramirez to light candles and leave her *regalos* on the sand and in the sea. *Olas de hermosas holas. Horneros. Y hombres excepcionales.*

Guapos. Guapas. Gauchos. And *Goooooooooooooooooooool!* We've gotten to

Fútbol! And I've become a fanatic. *Ya fui a mi* first *clasico,* between Peñarol y Nacional, and now only lack one task to becoming unofficially Uruguayan – learning to play *truco* – but of my fondness for the other game... obviously it has a lot to do with *futbolistas. Fainá. Y bueno ta, no falta mucho por al fin,* and

Everything yet to be said yet an expression of some sorts shared. *Empanadas.* I don't know if Uruguay invented the *tango* or *empanadas,* but it has perfected them.

Desfiles of diversity and marches for more *derechos humanos*, and the country is already known to be the most humanitarian in the Americas. The first country in the world to legalize marijuana, the first country to allow a woman to file for divorce, one of the few Latin American countries where abortion is safe and legal. Gay marriage, *claro*, like it was ever a question. Uruguay elected a transgender senator and has had two female vice presidents.

Chorizos, choripán, chivitos! But *Che, escúchame*, the way Italian, Spanish, and African genes have mixed with *los Charrua*.

Carne, the best meat in the world. Happy cows and 42 cuts of beef: *pulpón, asado, entrecot, lomo, nalga, peceto, vacío, colita de cuadril, morcilla* sweet or salty, *chinchulín, chorizo.* I dated a *carnicero.* I dated a cowboy. Carnival drums and *murgas*, parades and *bailarinas, las comparsas, la cumparsita*, a never-ending series of *cenas* and *cumples.*

But because the rhythm of the place I say, because the people: because the food, which centers on the

Asado, the barbecue, and ends with *aplausos* for the *asador.*

SAN SEBASTIAN, KNIGHT OF SWORDS

Sebastian the father   San Sebastian the son

/ rendered

Remember me   –   dumb

\ wordless

/ tongue-tied

Me   San Sebastian

\ strung

We leaned against the drunk stick tree

/ conversation

A mute I desired

\ conversion

/ armored archer

San Sebastian knight

/ of arrows

\ full   as an urchin

\ full of pricks

San Sebastian gentleman   Corded magician

         / & dumbstruck

Pricked bound   San Sebastian

       \ shouting Sebastian

Sebastian we could call it religion

            / love

     But let's call it

        \ rope

San Vladímir, The Keeper

saint vladimir was a name for the future
as if he were a well   vladímir

un timoto befriending an indian
summering the part of it mentioned

saint vladimir   another man inaugurated
san vladímir   the reason the moon returns

a drawing of breath   the wide horizon
at times   my only faith in god

THERE IS NO SAN LENÍN

i know there's no blue prince
like the beast of the apocalypse removed

separated by mountain chains   lenín
is my revolution*   my destination

into the clouds   of his name
an all-ism forcing me into exile

lenín is thirst and craving
is the human man made true

       Λ   Λ   Λ   Λ

and what fat chance this
cumulus sundry sums a bold thing lofty

enough to break regimen   situated
in the garden of theoretical significance

the gocho is wearing an unusual hat
el timotocuica is bright and shy

*because of his revolutionary activities
lenín is exempt from sainthood

PART II
HOME CATECHISM

THE HEAT RUN

VII

That slip in the shower was just enough aquajet punishment on the dwindling blossom to warm back into the frenzy. Washed hot toward the hip shimmy and shoulder dig. Sit. Down. Stay.

VI

Manic spin of new macho. Pre-everything sniff. Pre-bite. Pre-jump, pre-squat, pre-one leg lifted or stand still and stream. Mark your territory, mark my territory. And thrust just dominance. A dance to balance the whump and bark of preteen masturbation. Everything growl. Everything purr. Everything whine.

V

Off leash in a mile high tailspin. Undiapered into iced quicksand. Mountain trail lain down and maintained, browsed, parked. Mud carpet and overhang green. Solar windfields and sunflower screens. Blood pooling from a leg-shaking sleep but the comforter resoluble. Humanology floorboarded. The pull. The whistle. The stone.

IV

Hotel dramaturges extending corded autos: Salinas. Back at the back of the Days Inn. Kennelled and concreted. Cabbaged. The opposite of prairied. Deflocked and almost desoldiered. Beet-juiced bedspread and eight blankets of credit. Suddenly breasts, suddenly perked, suddenly root-vegged.

III

Little knots tangling, nerves ripening, some kind of delivery and an out of the car giddiness, day ending in Little Rock. First roadside full bloom and this city outskirt no safer than the panhandle. The carsick trick bullshit and good-natured sportiness jetlagged, those Easter nieces not sticking to anything with their sweet fingers and rabbit baskets. Squirrels! Another road this truck packed looking serious. One dog looking like coops are for chickens and at the same time where's my coop? This trip unsanctioned and ripped into winter, run wasted on window wheels along the Mississippi. That delta all swampland. All mystery.

II

Blood running cho-cho-cho-cho-co-co-colate. Choclo. Maíz. This in and out a maze of English and Spanish and this southern version of North America dizzying. Even a dog knows the rain drained counterclockwise and now this magnetic pull of centrifugal forest farmland and somehow my family, those nephews almost familiar, those dark haired tías, la abuela con sus árboles de pecan.

I

Starting from swamp, like a creation story – thirty minutes in customs and we come out Americans, that crate of detention to rental car, a phew of confusion lifted into daybreaking Everglades, sun coming up carp, coming up crawfish, mudpuppy me – rising from overnight jail stories, canines in flight purgatory, this breakfast a birth renewed and spring nation thickening into maturity, my blood-rich beginning cellular, four-footed, fin-and-gilled. Beak-boldened. Song-throated: Here I could sing. And but for my fathers, I would feed alligators.

THE OTHER FOOT

He came to church straight from the stomp dance
Wearing moccasins under his wedding dress.

Bearded, belled and turtle-shelled
He wore moccasins under his wedding dress.

His soul caught its own particular heart murmur
Wearing moccasins under his wedding dress.

Restless wakingtapping hum
He wore moccasins under his wedding dress.

Rim shot   rum shot   southern drum
Wearing moccasins under his wedding dress.

First time he loved anyone
He wore moccasins under his wedding dress.

52 Hawks

driving through muskogee, highway 62
is barbed wire. impossible not to mention
matthew shepard. not to mention orlando.

dusk silenced, we fuck in the vw
to prove something, we're alive at least,
and long enough to drain the car battery.

sleep then wake to a nightstick.
good luck, a good cop's jumpstart
from a dawn mourning too red. the hawk

must be a sign. you miss its flight, miss
the next one. there, i point. but you are reading
on your cell phone. obituaries. another raptor.

then a kind of rapture in the wish i make
out loud: a hawk to land on a fencepost. we begin
to count. one: you read stanley almodovar.

hawk two salutes: amanda alvear.
hawk three: oscar aracena-montero.
the hawks sentinel the road like honor

guards. 49 in six miles. they are something
we sing out names to. rudolfo. antonio.
darryl. angel. juan. luis. 49 hawks

and a morning full as a dance floor.
the 50th, a falcon, we call matthew
and quit our haunting inventory.

i metal the vw toward i-44
to flee the prairie purgatory. two birds on air,
there. you see and name us: not missing.

Stadium Mocs

side   to   side
       the moccasins slide-shuffle

left then right
       in the round dance

the toe   and heel
       of the chicken dance

these mocs   flex   and   stretch
      to   the   orange   rim   of
          the don't get me started
          on the hoop dance

my sneak-up shoes are the same as my stadium mocs

      I don't hear the ref's whistle to stop
      just the emcee's call for another intertribal

ODE TO THE CULEBRA

O snakes! And snakes I refrain
the tug of lifting you, restrain
the pull of your symbolic twist
my promise and my contradictions
mulled in scale of your constrictions
arm stained blue bicep to wrist

though happy I, young herpetologist
at reptile camp, rare Florida indigo
in my bare hands:
chimney doppler graveyard shift

we captured and were captivated
adolescent braves
addicted coarse cold-blooded
venom-blamed unsaved
and shedding skin intoxicating

negotiated year by year
my treaty with snakes
a compact not to interfere
with their directions or their homing aches

we're choosing paths and being chosen
poisoned penned untouched unspoken

What Shivers Since the Wheel Forgave Us

Our stuck tongues screamed louder
In Alabama, words hung in a rhythm

Reservation hands could basket
Tied back rocks rose, picked

Tarnished cigarettes unsupervised
Tucked between tobacco choruses

The stick figure beautifully contorted
Across drum and caught motioning

Toward a post-authentic
Grinning the words undressed

To out-sparked historians
Trading them the dance we packed

For breakfast, hands out-fished
Bent past our crane feathers

And Oklahoma over there imagined
Stretched and carved and reported

Magic from god dollars
No promised sounds abundant

Bays silent, the rinsed spirit singing
Thought + thought + thought

BACKYARD BLUE

he favored you after school   behind the church   in the shed converted
to weight room   discarding his polo and the god he loved   and you
understanding connection electric   your flesh word   a socket screamed
clear of infidelity   eyes lost on where the altar should be   the badge
the cross   his body   your body   the bench press
the minister tapping his feet   as he patched your devotion in tithing
your pocket   his teeth   his story   made your mouth raw

A Faster Scalpel

A house will bend, but pride holds me close.
He was the forearm of our transferred dark,

morose flesh one loomed to adventure.
My complexion kicked till it whitened.

I watched him watch his women, watch me.
I watched the explosion turn chaos

and the figure he played of you, you
carried through the collapsed family,

a bed dressed plump, and gracious
the faster scalpel. Señor noticed it was you,

me, noise, people, their rumors of a sky
to see hope in, an anesthetic mother

who thought that wood a friend's casket,
you who pulled gossip away

to some pressed locked parlor.
I plowed toward his bedroom, his want

told around the tender you pet
as bereavement, as rebellion full.

His eyes took the will of life. They stayed
peeled to the constant broke of abandon.

To death, Mother, he will save me
and loose us from the bones of anatomy.

Everyone talking conquests, Quiet.
Make something of your torture.

The Bells – Uranus Direct

This was it, logic presenting itself, eleventh grade Mrs. Wills' English class.

Uranus's perfect path, an entrepreneurial thought, the transfer student sculpted like Adonis.

Rite's passage and a lighthouse vow: Best friends digest rare conditions.

Including this eclipse-brought revelation.

The Baptist bodybuilder at sixteen iridescent.

A homework excuse, a pep rally party.

Rattling a nervous mother.

Suspicious rhythms in the paneled walls.

Of the light within light.

Of the bells

        the bells

        the bells

        the bells

        the bells

To a Secret Death

Your brother hid the will   flinched himself
loose of Christmas   of depth to the anatomy
every one of them talking you into Amanda
who slept ripped against her conquests

dream sissy come over   get it off your chest
her face against the wall   the riots seconding
your market   the back of opened Amanda
a darkening coffin   and something like torture

at each unbuttoning   stop Amanda
just this piece of shirt   she is in your class
was it your father   sharp sound

beside you   ripping you a new one
through family science   leave your shirt on
heart between surgeries   wince the awareness
embalming you you name animals

to break her   looking to those who look on
and the perverse love you persevere
arms raised in a cross   smoking the pregnancy
the raw body brown   the lit up took from her

she went to your school
father taught in the woodshop
crumbling the textbook of rebuttal
not this child   not this feeding

COULD BE YOU

Could be you at 17 preening.
Could be you frat boy, trying to think about _____.

Could be you soft athlete.
Could be your beer can pyramid.

Could be you one of those Indian boys missing.
Could be you still looking for trouble.

Could be your jaw behind the shin bone.
Could be you in the graveyard.

Rattle in Wetumpka

There's a rattle in Wetumpka, a rattle in my skin
Casino Indians pitching *Heys*, they're tipping bone and chin
They're digging up the ancestors, enrolling cowboys kin
There's a rattle in Wetumpka, a rattle in my skin
A coffin built with twenty floors, their souls to ante in
The Coosa River creeks will rise, and that's how it begins
There's a rattle in Wetumpka, a rattle in my skin
Casino Indians pitching *Heys*, they're chipping clay and chin

Seed Bead

unexpected sign I know exactly what to do with
unexpected sign I know exactly what it means

as oval as a tangerine   as orange
as ochre clay and sand

paint for an eye   another eye   another eye
protection from a what I knew was due

patio plumas palomas   reminder who
Sussanah Hosford   *Hadjo Pokke*

plastic seed bead   gift from above
gift from a bird reminder to

PICNIC FEATHERS

softened hours stirred
and cane encroaching
tobacco   the ankle drum

remembered lives finger hellos
climb afoot   turn heads
circle quietly

my grandfather walked god by the wrist
he rode wolves
his hands were mossy

A Real Cadillac

it was only seen from the stars
lined up   the one on the end garnishing
the sweat-slicked exhibition   facing away
removed   spared no scars or game

in front with the white front   he was
a different color scheme   locked from his left
inverted and expected race   recovered race
race you back to sleep

she hadn't told him she'd be behind them   behind her
back to let it all seem a hands-on fashion accessory
touched up by the old mosaic   laughing
to translate exactly   the stranger settled into the seats

stubble on the moonlit baptism
a scruffy feeling she wanted to shave
white hot she wanted him
lips heading downhill   she understood

replication   a cord around the exhibition
she kept the fabricated part of the day quiet
as promised   two high-stemmed glasses
she lay back in a real cadillac   she made love

to the eternal adornment of his headdress
the waterfront reminded her of sunrise service
the spring giving surprises   not everything determined
a spider's web over a shadow and the door

four inches from foreign   to turn out a visitor
to evoke abs woven together   the stitches pushed open
where two blue stones hung like the first arrival

C D Who I G L B

We arrived at the sun and I strayed in dark blond loops.
See the blanket at the dramatic point of the night. See
where I spread out. Yes and lay back and squatted down.

See how many shadows float on his shoulders. I nested up
from his glasses. He wasn't the Atlantic. The wind pulled
me back to the weather of colored pills.

I knew a quarter full and he was gentle as they rehabilitated him,
the blood red cowboy. See him through the capped needles
where he can't comfortably lie down or turn away.

A coincidence hippied up – the wind again cold enough
from the other Indians – its force like dull metal. It winded me.
We cleaned out the Old Testament.

From the garden dirt and cowboy in the house
to the arena at twelve, where I saw the tourist trap
and tomorrow. We hooked up to tiny flowers.

I heard the gasp of playing cards.
My mouth bordered the asphalt. The extra bed.
I bet and raised him my tradition.

THE MAGICIANS' TWINS

were expected to be easy to put down
expected to use tricks to make our parents think
they'd done wonderful things   expected

to evolve this sense of wonder and mystery
into more powerful a feeling than magicians
had felt before   to be a fantasy in the best tradition

of the game   magnetism and other related arts
such as antagonisms over the paranormal
expected to make things disappear and reappear

to make miracles out of nonsense banal   to confuse
the frontiers of science   we were expected
to compile our activities in a notebook

expected to be linked to community purpose
we were not expected to languish
we were expected to vanish

Part III
Saints of the Republic

WAR PORNOGRAPHY

What's the seduction of a weapon so massive it's capable of penetrating every bedroom in America? It's not poetry. But jacking off to violence so real it's almost like a movie. Republicans complain of Hollywood's abuse, but they've got a war sponsored by Kodak, Coca-Cola, and Uncle Scrooge's theme park, ejaculating the American way down throats palmed to swallow. And CNN pans a tan landscape of desert sand (or maybe it's filtered Malibu) zooming in on a dune that looks like a man lying on his side, and shading his eyes as he stares across the haze toward a land he dreams of making love to. He thinks he deserves a piece of her ass; after all he's risking his, over God's and Allah's big joke, good one too, hiding U.S. oil under Iraq. Fires light up smoky skies and, foreplay's over, here comes the real media fuck, so get your condoms, might as well seal 'em on with duct tape – and not just any silver-backed adhesive but Duck brand – because this situation will get even more explosive. The terror threat is now at Level Red. The feds have got it down, how to rev us up, but just before they get us off, this interruption: "Bally Total Fitness only $19 a month." I wonder what Iraqi television advertised before the Allies brought them Freedom Fries, the Church of Jesus Christ of Latter-day Saints, and most important, Exercise. Because McDonald's lies will pad Iraqi women's thighs and Uncle Sam wants them to exchange their burkas for Spandex and spread 'em. Ankles away. And strike my match, it's back. Conflict addictive as part-time ass. Well-developed victory battles illuminate the face of a soldier, a pilot, a prisoner, a journalist. Wrists remote-sore, eyes blurry, palms hairy. Forget when the war will end. Mount and ride the U.S. Constant Nymph Network. Or turn off the TV and fuck for peace.

Finding Love in Chelsea

To the right of the porn star & just above the drag queen,
You go-go-boyed on roller skates, when
I saw your picture in the back of *HX* magazine.

As Rollerboy you made the backpage weekend SEEN,
Pointed out by a love-rich, ill-read friend,
To the right of the porn star & just above the drag queen.

Knowing better, I asked how old. He smiled & said 19,
Then added that you go for older men.
That put a different spin on your picture in the *HX* magazine.

So young & yet already deviating from the mean,
Your leather jock & harness touting S&M,
To the right of the porn star & just above the drag queen.

I got your number & we did the blind date scene.
I liked you even better in the skin.
That picture didn't do you justice in the back of *HX* magazine.

Six months later & we'd just passed Halloween.
My friend had ripped the page out once again.
I checked out the porn stars & marveled at the drag queens.
Then I saw our picture on the back of *HX* magazine.

I Remember Joe Brainard's Cock Pics

I remember the first time I saw Joe Brainard's cock pics.
His lover Kenward kept a box and I was Kenward's
curious assistant. The cock was lovely, the photos keepers,
the sentiment a reminder things don't change much.
I've traded such with loves and lovers and strangers.
We seek revelations, and seeing Joe's cock was a revelation, a look

deeper into his art, somehow, his erotic art especially, a look
at his relationship with Kenward through printed black and white pics,
snapshots kept in a box on a shelf not shared with strangers,
though they're likely public now, sent and stored with Kenward's
papers at the University of California San Diego Library, so much
for cocksure anonymity in any age, at any age, dead or alive, and no secrets kept

in a world penned, painted and photographed by New York School poets who kept
and keep sharing each other's art and private lives for others to look
at and into through language and visuals. Not much
is hidden of Joe – tan crisp, cock long and thick, balls heavy – in these pics,
although he sports a skin-tight, tie-dyed tank top. It was the cool kind of strange
to realize these were all 1960s originals, photographed in Kenward's

Vermont bedroom. Joe's arms are crossed in front of and behind him. Kenward's
not the best photographer and has cropped off the top of Joe's head, keeping
his focus below the thick brown eyebrows, on his young god's goods. Joe's look
is bored and curious, a soft pout proud and pensive and strangely
both pornographic and poetic. Kenward's shots are amateur, without so much
consideration as to clean up the background. In one picture

there is laundry on the rocking chair. Another pic
Joe's sitting on the same rocking chair, his underwear thrown on Kenward's
bedroom floor, next to the coiled rug, where never very much
has been swept under. Of course I looked at Joe's cock – it was Joe Brainard's cock! –
but I kept
seeing the whitest thing in the black and white photograph. I kept looking
at the briefs crumbled on the floor, knowing with the strangest

sensation that I'd seen the same white shape before, although myself no stranger
to underwear quickly tossed disrobing for a lover or to send a potential lover a hasty
unedited pic.
I carried the picture along Kenward's storied stairwell, among Joe's art, looking
for the image I knew I'd seen before, framed among Kenward's
collection walls. I found it: Joe's lightly penciled pair of crumbled paper briefs. I kept
comparing the pic with the white collage, confirming a photo-to-art match.

I admit to admiring Kenward's collection of Joe's cock pics,
kept undisclosed for more than 50 years, stored now I suppose with so much
boxed material sent to UCSD. It's strange what you might find when you know where
to look.

Guzzling Hafiz

The gag was tight across his mouth
At first, to save his crying out his mouth

No way to thank his master's service then
But taking in whatever came about his mouth

His master's P.A.'ed prick would piss
Inside his ass without his mouth

Cock proven, he'd been slave traded
No owner ever had to doubt his mouth

This master had paraded him
On Folsom Street, had rented out his mouth

And while his ass was tendered only by his Sir
Sir touted any hairy lout to rout his mouth

They toured Nasty Pig events in Amsterdam
Had porn producers scout his mouth

Hafiz praised those stardust days of ludes
And taking loads until his Sir licked out his mouth

My Master Hafiz, I should say, who's leading me
And doesn't know where we would be today without his mouth

PISS & VINEGAR

(after Tim Dlugos)

Cut	Uncut
Top	Bottom
West Village	Lower East Side
Rome	Paris
Cigarettes	Crystal
Yoga	Push-ups
P.C.	P.A.
Snowboard	Skateboard
Rapture Salad	Milanesa
Piss	Pits
Blue	Brown
Brown	Black
Black	Con Leche
Distracted	Distracted
Manu Chao	Babasonicos
Forty	Twenty-eight
Banana	Salvation
Calvin	Lupo
Paper wallets	Clay dolls
Tim Dlugos	Julio Cortázar
Ft. Walton Beach	Montevideo
Espresso	Yerba Mate
Goat	Goat
Malbec	Malbec
Pot	Pot
Speedo	Speed

Manifesto – Mercury Direct

I was actually looking forward
to this coming Mercury retrograde.
I wanted things to go back
to their normal miscommunications. I played

my country music records backwards,
wrote a How To Remove Anger spell,
I even went to the seventh plane of existence to
release our soul fragments and wrote an old-fashioned letter to tell

you how sorry I was for
ever letting this grand misunderstanding
stalemate into something that grew against
all sense of reason. But I also couldn't see defending

the man I thought you knew so well
from all the lies you threw
in your responding email. I thought it was unhealthy
to itemize each error and prove what each of us already knew

to be untrue, to let those things lie,
as they say, a while longer. But how long
and how come and why does the fact
that I find the rights among the wrongs

you catalog among my given rights
in being human, a man, and not to mention your exboyfriend
bother me? Though you were right to list the responsibilities
you required from me as your friend

despite omitting all that I'd already been,
for now I knew what I had not been living
up to in your eyes and what I'd have to be
like, "human," for you to see me in that kind of light again. I'm not giving

up, or giving in, but only giving
you the space I've needed when you
need it now. Language is a barrier that takes
relationships for granted, and yes, it's true

I thought nothing would ever come
of us, but nor between us, until your perjury
became testimony you believed, leaving
me with the effects of the directness of Mercury.

IRREGULAR GRATITUDE: THE PREACHER AND THE PROSTITUTE

for Ted Haggard & Mike Jones

ted: the chemist converted finds laying a man absorbs attentive meanness
mike: allows every clergyman his time to have cheerfulness

ted: some pain for money   for well-appointed carriage
mike: some joy best voluntarily   unhinged

ted: what access and ways into plain-dealing people
mike: glimpses widen doors   theories unscientific

ted: we have an element of friendship
mike: we have a good deal little angel

June 26, 2015

When you became my groom, we were both grooms.
In a room hallowed by justice, just us benedicted.
Does a first kiss in a graveyard foreshadow Till death?
Surprised by the Supreme Court's decision if not our fathers'

Benediction in a room hallowed by justice. Just us
Professional grooms, tailor-made for TV interviews.
Were we surprised by the Supreme Court's historic decision?
What a wedding gift. Galvanized. Who chose the day?

Groomed by professionals, tailored, interviewed for TV news.
Old rings our fathers' heirlooms hammered new.
What wedding gifts. Galvanized. An historic day.
Friends stand in for family, which is as good as God.

And the rings our fathers' heirlooms hammered new.
When you became my groom, we were both grooms.
Chosen in front of family, which is better than God.
Our first kiss in a graveyard. It foreshadowed justice.

K's Cloud

for James Schuyler

a gray day by the breakfast lilies
your Ninnies' Nest dog-eared
the bed you dug to bury
dirty money panes away

ferning into low clouds
spider grass spidering
invisible Veronica Lake
H drove you to hosp

K's fat fingers clasp the big Z
tap the early 1970s
palsy-stained paperback

There was drinking in the carriage
There was a house joint
Now not a leaf turns
But there is a cloud

Birds of Cain

blinded by divine rejection

perhaps their most fundamental characteristic

they were almost eagles

emblematic inhabitants of human mythology

yet we know almost nothing about them

sullen raptors official keepers

usually fanned out in flight

of jealousy brought to the limelight

wings cocked the birds of cain

continent to the east

are leading the exodus

continent to the north

feathered truants used metaphorically

continent to the west

to represent chaos and the presence of evil

continent to the south

they are practicing sidewards remorse

one of five animals of the vernal equinox

and mute except to hiss and grunt

artilleries targeting correction

the birds of cain are not responsible

certainly not in a neighborly way

for the content of any material

synonymous with terms applied to lovers

encountered after leaving this page

last of the scavengers surviving our century

via link or otherwise

social soarers

gathered in flocks

quitting earth

SAINTS OF THE REPUBLIC

There have been so many gods of love
Eras of religious eros   heroes
Studded in celestial exhalation

Examining the exultations missed
And advantaged   exalting questions
Interpreted secular   erogenous excess

Sects dedicated to eros   heroic
Exaltations   anatomical devotions
There are so many gods of love

ACKNOWLEDGMENTS

Thanks/Gracias to Kenward Elmslie, Ron Padgett, Ai, Linda Hogan, Joy Harjo, Lucia Berlin, Charles Dearmond, Lauren Myers, L.S Asekoff, Nicolas Arellano, Kimberly Becker, Carolina De Robertis, Juan Ros, Silvia Carrero Parris, Lenín Gomez, Spuyten Duyvil, Brooklyn College, Institute of American Indian Arts, y la República Oriental del Uruguay.

Millones de gracias to Gabriel Insiburo for a thousand reasons, including the permission to use his photo collage "Nico" on this book's cover, in which the model's crown/halo is formed with a stanza from Juana de Ibarbourou's poem "El Dulce Milagro."

Thank you to the editors and readers of the following journals and anthologies where poems
from *Saints of the Republic* originally appeared:

Palo Borracho; **San Benito**, There is no San Lenín, *Poem A Day series,*
   Academy of American Poets;
San Vitalis of Fetishes, *Fourteen Hills*;
San Timotheo's Line, NYQuarterly's *Leap of Faith* anthology;
Santos de la República, *Hairstreak Butterfly Review*;
Las Llamadas, *Copihue Poetry*;
San Judas Tadeo; **Ode to the Culebra**, *Juked Poetry*;
Sans Justus, The Martyrs; **San Sebastian**, **Knight of Swords**, *New American Writing*;
The Alphabet of the Republic, *Carve*;
The Heat Run, *Animal*;
The Other Foot, *Cincinnati Review*;
52 Hawks; **June 26, 2015**, *Kestrel*;
Stadium Mocs, *Prairie Schooner*; *Bodies Built for Game* anthology;
What Shivers Since the Wheel Forgave Us; **A Real Cadillac**, *World Literature Today*;
Backyard Blue; **Birds of Cain**; **picnic feathers**, *Yellow Medicine Review*;
A Faster Scalpel; **Piss & Vinegar**, *Cutbank*;
To a Secret Death, *Hinchas de Poesia*;
Seed Bead, *The Journal*;
Rattle in Wetumpka; **Finding Love in Chelsea**, *Barrow Street*;
Could Be You, *Codex*;
The Magicians' Twins, *Poet Lore*;
War Pornography, *Hazmat Review*;
I Remember Joe Brainard's Cock Pics, *Punctuate*; *LoveJets* anthology;
Guzzling Hafiz, *Bloom*; *Stonewall's Legacy* anthology;
Manifesto, Mercury Direct, *Toe Good Poetry*;
Irregular Gratitude, *ALARUM*;
K's Cloud, *Anomaly, Verse Daily*;
Saints of the Republic, *Lambda Literary Spotlight*.

CHIP LIVINGSTON is a queer/two-spirit, mixed-blood Creek writer and the author of two previous collections of poetry, *Crow-Blue, Crow-Black* and *Museum of False Starts*, as well as a chapbook of poems, a novel, and a short story/essay collection. He is the editor of *Love, Loosha: The Letters of Lucia Berlin and Kenward Elmslie*. Chip teaches in the low-rez MFA program at the Institute of American Indian Arts in Santa Fe, New Mexico. He lives in Montevideo, Uruguay.

www.ingramcontent.com/pod-product-compliance
Lightning Source LLC
Chambersburg PA
CBHW041519120626
46551CB00018B/2492